NO ONE IS **GOOD** EXCEPT **GOD ALONE**

God's Ultimatum for the Church to
Pierce through Darkness
Defeat Evil
Conquer the World

HANH NGUYEN

ISBN: 979-8-89109-708-7 - paperback
ISBN: 979-8-89109-709-4 - ebook

Contents

ACKNOWLEDGMENT

This book cannot exist without amazing blessing from my Heavenly Father in every aspect, every stage to its finished production.

I am deeply grateful to my Heavenly Father for the revelation of the knowledge of His Goodness and the wisdom to implement divine insights into this book.

I am grateful for specially skillful and dedicating people who helped me with the production of the book:

- Karen Pina and the book production team of Self-Publishing School for coaching, arranging materials and publishing,
- Gregory Baker for proofreading and editing the manuscript.

INTRODUCTION

What is good and what is evil? What is the foundational standard for your judgment of what is good and what is evil? The world is in turmoil with a clash of opinions about what is really good and evil. Cultures in many countries have changed dramatically to the point of reversing the norm of good and evil so that what once was considered good is now evil and what was once known as evil is now good. This twisting of the meaning of good and evil is invading cultures through many avenues, especially through media, through communication systems, and worst of all through the education system. People from previous generations cannot accept this new wave of conception about good and evil without searing their conscience with striking agony.

In reality, the acceptable understanding of good and evil is not 100% received by any generation. Undeniable confusion has reigned throughout history since the Fall. When Adam and Eve ate the fruit from the tree of the knowledge of good and evil, expecting to gain this knowledge, they instead were cut off from the Goodness of God, and the seed of confusion was planted in their hearts.

But God did not create man in His image to be locked in confusion. There is no confusion in God, and there should be no confusion in man. He knows very well what is good and what is evil based on the standard of His Own Goodness. Only through the knowledge of the Goodness of God can man judge with absolute confidence what is good and what is evil. Indeed, when done by that standard, no one, no argument, no debate, no temptation, no threat, no operation, and no government can deter them from their stand. As God set the value of life based on the standard of His Goodness, so must we frame society in the same model of His Kingdom culture.

Just like many other Christians, I share the same concern and frustration over the invasion of anti-biblical programs and projects that overtly defy all Christian values that we have known and respected. Just like many other Christians, I recognize the need for serious prayers with fervent longing for God's answer. But I may be among the few who did not tell God what I expect Him to do. Instead, I remained still to know that He is God (Psalm 46:10), to stand at my watch and see what He would say to me (Habakkuk 2:1), and to write down the revelation according to His instruction (Habakkuk 2:2). I have followed the *4Keys of Hearing God's Voice* by Dr. Virkler's teaching as I attended Christian Leadership University for my doctoral degree. This book is the result of my three-year devotion and journaling.

I have learned that there is no more important knowledge of God than that of His Goodness. All theology must be based on the foundation of His Goodness. Every teaching that steers away from His Goodness is demonic and unacceptable, and no matter how flattering it is to the ears, how logical it sounds to the mind, or how convincing it presses on the heart, it is false doctrine. It's time that

God's people know His Goodness in their hearts and understand it through their experiences.

This book presents a beautiful display of the magnificent scenery of God's Goodness, much like the perfect garden with the Tree of Life, promised lands, rivers of living water, heavenly sky, and the roadmap to the Kingdom of God. It is up to every reader to paint this picture on the canvas of his or her life to fulfill his or her destiny so that the Kingdom of God may come and His will be done on earth as it is in heaven.

CHAPTER 1

THE RICH MAN WANTED THE KINGDOM OF GOD

Mark 10:17-18 – *17 As He was setting out on a journey, a man ran up to Him and knelt before Him, and asked Him, "Good Teacher, what shall I do to inherit eternal life?" 18 And Jesus said to him, "Why do you call Me good? No one is good except God alone.*

THE RICH MAN was successful in every way. He held a high position in the society to which he belonged (Luke 18:18). He gained respect, he was significant, and he achieved significant recognition in the world in which he lived. He was satisfied in his soul. Concerning material life, he was rich, he was wealthy (Luke 18:23), and he was above needs. Surely, there was no lack in his physical satisfaction. Spiritually, he had a heart for God. He feared God, he respected God, and he was serious in living his life in line with God's law as he was taught (Luke 18:20-21). He knew that there was a Kingdom beyond this world, the one he knew existed and wanted to see and interact with. The great thing about this man was that, regardless of all his achievement and possession on earth, he was well aware that they still could not guarantee his inheritance of the Kingdom because they could not match the standard of

God's Kingdom. Nothing coming from this earth can qualify you for access to God's Kingdom.

Surely, success and earthly virtue cannot guarantee entrance to the Kingdom of God.

So, he came to Jesus, Who had nothing resembling what the rich man had earned in the prime of his life. Jesus did not have a place to lay His head (Luke 9:58), He did not own anything in His name, He did not hold any religious and political position in the Jewish government, and He was not among the elite society. Yet, His lifestyle was superior to the highest ranking of social hierarchy of the day. Though He was not among the accredited Jewish religious leaders, yet His teachings were amazing and authoritative in ways that people had never heard before.

Surely, success and earthly virtue cannot guarantee entrance to the Kingdom of God.

> Luke 4:31-32 (TPT) – *³¹ Jesus went to Capernaum in Galilee and taught the people on the Sabbath day. ³² His teachings stunned and dazed them, for he spoke with penetrating words and great authority.*

All His teachings focused on the Kingdom and were accompanied with demonstrations of signs and wonders to meet people's needs and to direct their attention toward the Kingdom of God. Jesus' words and works indeed captivated people's hearts and stirred up their longing for the Kingdom of God, not just the needy, the poor, the sick, the demonized, but also the ones with sound minds and healthy and wealthy lifestyles.

The man asked Jesus what good deeds he should do to inherit eternal life, and Jesus told him that the goodness in the heart was more important. Now, talking about goodness, Jesus emphasized that only God is good, for there is no goodness in man. To such a heart seeking after the things of God, Jesus revealed deeper truth that has never entered the heart of man. The man should have seen all of Jesus' good deeds in words and works and called Him Good Teacher. But Jesus made it clear that man should not focus on good deeds alone but rather on the goodness in heart that motivated people to do good deeds. Man focus on deeds, but God focuses on the heart.

Don't just look at the good deeds to identify a person as good. We cannot judge a person by outside appearance or by their deeds but should seek further in the intention of the heart. It is very important that we know the

> *Man focus on deeds but God focuses on the heart.*

source of that goodness in order to know for sure that it is good. Only the Goodness of God is unconditional, for it does not need our return goodness, which is always conditional.

The rich man was wise, first because he feared God and he recognized his humble position toward God. Second, he was a wise man because he recognized that Jesus came from the Kingdom, and he knew that He had the answer to the quest of his heart's yearning. He was a wise man with the gift of discernment to know where to find the well that sprang up with living water that could quench his thirst for the Kingdom. He was wise not to risk his inheritance of the Kingdom with the temporary pride of this world.

If you know that you are wise, this book is for you. If you believe you are wise, this book is for you. If you think you are wise, this book is for you. If you are wise and you are a leader at any level, an older brother or sister, a parent, a teacher, an officer, a CEO, a COO, a CFO, a president of any organization, especially in education, or if you are a leader in business, in government, or in ministry, then this book is for you. If you think you don't belong to any of these, I suggest that you quiet yourself and listen to your heart, because wisdom is in the heart.

Deep down, in every man's heart, is a yearning for true Goodness that originates from the Kingdom of God. Goodness has to come from God's Kingdom for man to be qualified to enter His Kingdom. Such Goodness you cannot find in this world because *no one is good except God alone*.

CHAPTER 2

NO ONE IS GOOD EXCEPT GOD ALONE

NO ONE IS GOOD except God alone! That statement brings so much freedom and revelation to humanity. First, it relieves us from the obligation to be good and do good, from the guilt of missing the mark, from self-condemnation, from self-pity, from envy and jealousy, from striving to match people's expectations, from seeking man's approval, from the illusion of self-righteousness, and from the trap of pride.

Second, it helps us release others from the obligation to be good and do good, from our expectations of them, from our anger of their missing the mark, from our accusation, condemnation, judgmentalism, from our shaming them for their lack, their poor performance, or their needs.

God alone is good. God is the source of Goodness. God alone set the standard of Goodness. Only God can model true Goodness. God alone can satisfy our yearning for Goodness. Goodness can only be found in God. Goodness can only be found in His presence. Compared to God's, man's goodness is futile and vain.

No one is good except God alone. That is clear enough. No one is good, so why do we try to do good if we are not good? We can want to be good, and we want to be good because we are made in God's image, but we cannot be good or do good because no one is good. Trying to be good or to do good is typical humanism.

Jesus' statement shows that God knows very well that man is not good. He does not expect us to be good or to be able to do good by ourselves. He does not demand us to be good and do good. He does not condemn us for being short of goodness. He knows that we need His help

Our calling is to show the world how good God is to lead people to Him.

and only the Good God can help us. Our goodness can be manifested through our good works and deeds, but true Goodness cannot be found in us. It should only come from God because only He is good. Our goodness should not come from us but from the Spirit of God in us.

Why did Jesus tell the rich man, "Why do you call Me good?" Because the man was focusing on man's power to do good. He had a heart to do good, desired to do good, and he had tried hard to be good by trying to obey all the laws possible. Jesus wanted to refocus him toward the source of Goodness: God. The reason Jesus did good was because God was in Him doing the work and He submitted Himself to His Father Who is good.

Like Jesus, we can receive God's Goodness, express God's Goodness, but, unlike Jesus, we cannot give His Goodness to anybody. In other words, we cannot make anybody good. We cannot rely on our way, our will, our wisdom, our ability to make anybody good. That is not our calling anyway. Out calling is not to show the world how good we are by pleasing people. Our calling is to show the world how good God is to lead people to Him.

To fulfill our calling, we need to know the difference between the Goodness of God and the goodness of man, or in another term, humanism.

CHAPTER 3

GOD'S GOODNESS VS. HUMANISM

THERE IS ONLY GOODNESS IN GOD. In Him there is no evil. He alone has good thoughts toward man (Jeremiah 29:11). He created man and placed him into a perfect environment, and His first command was for man to have dominion over His Creation. When man fell into the devil's trap of deception, He immediately revealed His plan of salvation through Jesus Christ that He had prepared even before the foundation of the earth (Ephesians 1:4-5). His plan was to bless mankind and not to condemn them. Condemnation comes from the law and not from His will and His plan and purpose for mankind.

God has great intention to lavish man with His best blessings, ones we cannot find anywhere else in this world. God has great plans and strategies to help man become successful and prosperous through and through. God alone can be our Savior. He alone is the Way of Life for all mankind.

Man, on the other hand, is both good and evil. There is no man on earth in whom we find no evil.

Romans 3:10 – *as it is written, THERE IS NONE RIGHTEOUS, NOT EVEN ONE;*

Romans 3:23 – *for all have sinned and fall short of the glory of God.*

Man's goodness and evil are found in their thoughts, emotions, desires, and decisions as they fluctuate with time and circumstances. They are fragile, inconsistent, easily broken, easily manipulated, easily fallen, and easily defeated. They are futile and vain in their attempts to be righteous, just, moral, to have value, and to have a life of virtue.

> Isaiah 64:6 – *For all of us have become like one who is unclean, And all our righteous deeds are like a filthy garment; And all of us wither like a leaf, And our iniquities, like the wind, take us away.*

Mankind is unreliable and incongruent in words and deeds, in promises, in business, and in ministries. In the end, they find themselves stuck in powerlessness where they succumb to circumstances, to sin, and become victimized and abused against their own will. The main problem is that man doesn't know the Goodness of God. Since the fall, man has been deceived by the goodness from the tree of the knowledge of good and evil.

God is good all the time, but man is not, because their hearts and minds are not stable toward God. Today, man can be purely good, but at other times, man shows a faulty humanistic goodness. They are not the same, because they are not from the same source and have the same motives. God's Goodness can only come from God, and the goal is to bless people. Man's goodness comes from self-righteousness or some natural or demonic source, and the goal is self-righteousness, no matter how sincere and sacrificial the deeds are.

True Goodness is not in the heart of man but in the essence of God.

God's Goodness does not come from man's goodness. A good man is not always a godly man. There should be no confusion between God's Goodness and man's goodness. One comes from the Tree of Life and leads to Life, the other comes from the tree of the knowledge of good and evil and leads to death.

True Goodness is not in the heart of man but in the essence of God.

There is Life in God's Goodness. God's Goodness is the Life-Giver. People die because of wickedness, but God's Goodness resurrects them and brings them Life abundantly. Sometimes, people have to taste death before they realize how desperately they need Life. Only then are they willing to surrender everything to gain His Life. That is when they can take up the cross and follow Jesus. Taking up the cross does not aim at making man suffer, but to kill the flesh and to remove humanism from man so that they can freely walk on the path of the Tree of Life. You can only choose one, because they don't cooperate or tolerate each other.

God's Goodness comes from the Tree of Life and not from the tree of the knowledge of good and evil. No one can be good, and no one can do good by following the tree of the knowledge of good and evil. No matter how well you know good and how well you know evil, you will not know God's Goodness as long as you walk on the path of the tree of the knowledge of good and evil. These are parallel paths that can never meet each other and, in fact, they head in opposite directions: one toward Life and one toward death. One gives Life, the other leads to death. One gives hope, the other pushes to desperation. One empowers faith, the other entraps people in fear.

The notion that all religions teach you to do good is a lie. Many people say such as an excuse to deny the salvation through Jesus Christ. That is surely satan's deception. However, God will not leave them in the hands of satan. His Truth always prevails and conquers.

God's Goodness is your promised land. God's Goodness is your green pastures. God's Goodness is your strong tower. Man's goodness provokes and legalizes the devil's attack upon people's lives. God's Goodness confronts and defeats the devil and all his tactics against mankind. God's Goodness does not legalize wickedness, but it quenches evil even before it shows up. Wickedness cannot stand in the presence of God's Goodness which does not exalt man but glorifies God.

> *Wickedness cannot stand in the presence of God's Goodness which does not exalt man but glorifies God.*

There is an obvious contrast between humanistic goodness and God's Goodness. People tend to look at your good deeds to either praise you out of admiration, which leads to pride, or to persecute you out of jealousy, which leads to strife. That's the consequences of humanistic goodness. God's Goodness never provokes jealousy and never promotes pride. Jealousy comes from outside and pride comes from inside, and both make you offensive to God and open to the devil. But when you walk in the Goodness of God, you can't offend God and you can't lose to the devil. God's Goodness is your protection in and out, up and down.

God loves you; God loves humanity, but God opposes humanism. Humanity came from God, but humanism came from the collaboration of man and the devil. Therefore, goodness in man is distorted, warped, and never accepted in the Kingdom of God.

God loves you; God loves humanity; but God opposes humanism.

God loves people coming to Him with the desire for an answer and not with a challenge of competition. No one can compete with God. No one can manipulate God. When you walk in God's Goodness, no one can influence you or manipulate you away from God. But when you walk in the pride of humanism, you are vulnerable to the fiery darts of the enemy, and you will become a casualty.

God loves to see His people come to Him in humility and poor in spirit and never in the pride of humanism. There is hope for the brokenhearted, there are open doors for the humbled, there is no denial for the seeking, and there is no rejection for the hopeful. All are invited and all are welcome to God's Kingdom because you will all be transformed into the image of Jesus, the First Born of the New Family of Righteousness and Justice. You are going to know God and enjoy Him as He always desires to see you in His shalom, and, with Him, all things are possible.

CHAPTER 4

ALL THINGS ARE POSSIBLE WITH GOD

Mark 10:19-27 – [19] *"You know the commandments, 'DO NOT MURDER, DO NOT COMMIT ADULTERY, DO NOT STEAL, DO NOT BEAR FALSE WITNESS, Do not defraud, HONOR YOUR FATHER AND MOTHER.'"* [20] *And he said to Him, "Teacher, I have kept all these things from my youth up."* [21] *Looking at him, Jesus felt a love for him and said to him. "One thing you lack: go and sell all you possess and give to the poor, and you will have treasure in heaven; and come, follow Me."* [22] *But at these words he was saddened, and he went away grieving for he was one who owned much property.* [23] *And Jesus, looking around, said to His disciples, "How hard it will be for those who are wealthy to enter the kingdom of God!"* [24] *The disciples were amazed at His words. But Jesus answered again and said to them, "Children, how hard it is to enter the kingdom of God!* [25] *It is easier for a camel to go through the eye of a needle than for a rich man to enter the kingdom of God."* [26] *They were even more astonished and said to Him, "Then who can be saved?"* [27] *Looking at them, Jesus said, "With people it is impossible, but not with God; for all things are possible with God."*

MANY OF GOD'S PEOPLE can identify themselves with the rich man because they too have tried hard to do good and be good in their Christian walk. They have attempted to keep a diligent Christian life with faithful reading of the Word, studying the Word, attending Bible study meetings, going to conferences, going to church, paying tithes, serving, ministering, teaching, preaching, worshipping, and praying. These are all familiar Christian activities that few miss. And yet, while trying hard to do everything one can think of to lead a good Christian life, deep down in every heart, there is the knowledge that something is missing, and it prickles his or her conscience and locks him or her in the uncertainty of salvation. Just like the rich man, Jesus can always draw out from each one of us something we failed in or something we are not willing to give up. The evidence of this is how we try to cover it and defend ourselves...by using the cliché, "I'm only human!"

As "we are human," we are rich in humanism! We are used to reacting in all situations by the goodness of man. Many can claim to be led by the Spirit of God, to do ministry by the power of the Spirit, but few ever claim to be led by the Goodness of God. Many can claim that they succeed by the Goodness of God, but how many can profess that they are compelled by the Goodness of God in their hearts to minister to people? How many can claim that they serve in the house of God out of the Goodness of God in their hearts?

The main opposition against the Goodness of God in our lives are wicked thoughts. They oppose and hinder the Goodness of God in our lives. The fertile soil for wicked thoughts is humanism, focusing on man, expecting man to be the source of your provision and protection. Humanism is wicked and evil. There is nothing good about humanism. Its goodness is like the world's angel of light: the devil (2 Corinthians 11:14).

God's beloved children, God wants to detox you from humanism. It is poisonous; it is the sting of death. It is the fruit of the tree of the knowledge of good and evil. As long as you eat this fruit, you are banned from the Tree of Life. How can you introduce people to the Kingdom of God when you yourself are banned from the Tree of Life?

Beloved children of God, walking the path of the Tree of Life does not require human effort. Actually, it does not even accept human effort. Rather, it calls for your decision to focus on Jesus and let Him do the work through you. With His Love in you, you can love easily. With His Goodness in you, you can be good to people regardless of their wickedness. Jesus is not afraid of the wicked; they cannot do anything against Him. In the end, they can only succumb to the power of His Love.

Jesus is not afraid of the wicked; they cannot do anything against Him. In the end, they can only succumb to the power of His Love.

Beloved children of God, your focus is not on trying to be good or do good. Your focus is on looking at Jesus, looking at His glory so that you may be transformed into His image. Whatever or whoever you focus on, you will take on their image, their assimilation. So, focus on Jesus—though you should be careful that your motivation is not on trying to make God look good. But once you truly focus on Jesus, you will be transformed into His image, and being good will come naturally to you. Focusing on Jesus frees you from humanism.

> **2 Corinthians 3:18** – *But we all, with unveiled face, beholding as in a mirror the glory of the Lord, are being transformed into the same image from glory to glory, just as from the Lord, the Spirit.*

When you stop relying on the goodness of man in you, when you recognize your goodness is just a filthy rag in God's sight (Isaiah 64:6), you release yourself from the impossibility of man. When you start to realize the omnipotence of the Goodness of God, you position yourself at the gate where "all things are possible with God." Surrender to God and He will refine you, clothe you, and fill you with spiritual wisdom and understanding to become as good as He is.

CHAPTER 5

HOW TO GROW IN THE GOODNESS OF GOD

Matthew 5:48 – *Therefore you are to be perfect, as your heavenly Father is perfect.*

The statement above is not a suggestion; it is a mandate for all Jesus' followers. Perfection can only be found in The Goodness of God which only comes from God, and it is pure and genuine and fruitful. To operate out of the Goodness of God without contamination of earthly, natural, and demonic motives, you need to have a genuine relationship with God. Surely, with God, you cannot have a fake relationship. It is not for God's sake but for your own sake that you seek to have a genuine relationship with God.

Your actual involvement is to submit yourself to Him, Who is good. It means that you consciously focus on the Good God and consult and rely on Him for everything you do. The reason you can obey Him is because you can trust Him. Why can you trust Him? Because you spend time with Him, you count His blessings on your life, and you focus on the positive things He has done in your life through comfort as well as in hardship of life. Daily communion gives you boldness to approach His throne of grace.

You cannot cook up the Goodness of God. You cannot conjure the Goodness of God. You can only receive the

Goodness of God passively by actively opening up yourself. The more you pray in the Spirit, the more you open yourself and your spirit resonates with the heavenly frequency of Life. You will be transformed. In fact, you are transforming.

You cannot cook up the Goodness of God. You cannot conjure the Goodness of God.

Pray in the Spirit and focus on the Kingdom. You are God's representative on earth, and you have the full support from His Kingdom. Pray in the Spirit at all times.

Everything that happens around you is to compel you to pray in the Spirit more steadily and frequently so that the conception of the eternal you will become a reality. This idea is not your opinion, it is God's inspiration. Persevere through, press more on praying in tongues. You are the chosen one. Chosen for what? For His glory to manifest on earth through you. Yes, that is God's Goodness. He is with you to equip you and fortify His Goodness in you. Only He can do this for you. Let your mind be occupied with God's Goodness so that His Spirit can guide you into all Truth and nothing will be able to deter you from Him anymore.

Simple assignment: pray in tongues more frequently and earnestly. Would you do that? Well, with His Spirit in you, you will. There is no self-effort needed. All you need to do is surrender to His Spirit.

As your spirit is in oneness with God, His Goodness just flows freely to you and from you so that you don't have to try to be good. You simply show His Goodness to people. If you have to use your mind to live out God's Goodness, then that is not His Goodness but your human goodness.

Anything from God flows spontaneously without the control of your mind. In short, you don't have to think to be good. What your mind should land on is Jesus, recognizing His presence in you.

When you focus on the good deeds you do, you are prone to pride and to the devil's tricks. Focus on the Holy Trinity. Focus on the Father's Love. Focus on the Son's Light. Focus on the Holy Spirit's Life. You can never go wrong with this.

Doing good to people should not be your focus. Your focus is on receiving and experiencing the Goodness of God. You will automatically or spontaneously give what you receive because His Life is a flowing river. The river of Life is not a lake or a pond. It is a river. Out of the abundance of your heart, you will speak and give—which is exactly how the Goodness of God will flow out from you.

Recognizing that God is good is not enough. You need to experience His Goodness to you, and then your faith grows and gives more room for His Goodness to be released to you.

Faith toward God is your next assignment. Continue to identify and remove dead works in your life so that you can totally walk in the path leading to the Tree of Life. God is on this journey with you. Now faith is the big issue which results in opening the door to all the rest. You have advanced a lot in faith, and you need to increase it yet more.

Faith is your ammunition to blow up doubt and destroy lies and strongholds completely. Faith is not like a broom to sweep dirt out of your house. Faith should be used to bombard the strongholds of darkness into rubble. Only the faith of God and faith toward God can fulfill this task. The more you spend time with God, not just at a set time for devotion, but throughout the day praying in the Spirit, the more you are able to focus on Him and the more you will be in tune with His Spirit. Indeed, the more you sow in the Spirit, the more the faith of God grows in you so that you can stand firm and steadfast on the faith toward God. The more you focus on God, the more He can flow through you to minister to people and take charge of the world.

Your faith to transform communities and conquer the world grows with God's DNA prevailing in you. Of course, you don't want to be good by forcing yourself to apply the "what would Jesus do?" (WWJD) mentality. God wants you to focus on Him and pray in the Spirit constantly, especially when you face temptation to yield to your flesh. Praying in the Spirit will keep your flesh dead. Humanism will resurrect your flesh because humanism is itself the flesh. All the works of humanism are dead works. You don't need faith to do dead works. You need faith to do Life-giving works, because you have to see beyond what you don't see now. You walk by faith because you don't see the thing you hope for yet, but you know that it is there in the spirit world and you speak it into existence to the physical world, bringing the heavenly reality to become physical reality.

You don't need faith to do dead works.

Yes, faith allows you to see the Goodness of God beyond your humanistic perception. The person who has faith is the one who can see the Goodness of God in all situations.

On the other hand, the fear of sin, the fear of committing sin, or the fear of falling into sin simply empowers sin to overtake you. Why? Because fear is the facilitator of darkness and the catalyst of sin. The knowledge of God's Love and having faith in His Grace empowers you to trust God and live dependently on Him. You will be released from the obligation to do good but will naturally do good because of the Good God in you. Whenever you face the temptation of sin, don't focus on your weakness or on the temptation, but redirect your focus on Jesus, and consciously yield yourself to Him. Pray and surrender to His Spirit. God is with you and is on your side. The fear of man is a trap. It ensnares His people into the sin of doubt, resulting in the falling away from His path of Life.

Fear is the facilitator of darkness and the catalyst of sin.

Goodness surely releases you from the fear of man and the guilt of hurting man. Many of you used to feel sorry and regret over what you have done. But when you start with the Goodness of God and do everything out of the Goodness of God, you don't have to fear man and their feelings, regardless of how they react. Let Goodness be the motivation of everything you do, and you will find grace and boldness to approach people with His Kingdom business.

In many cases, your anger may look like it is helping you force others to do what you want them to do, but it grows the root of bitterness underneath and provokes rebellion. When you yield yourself to Jesus, you release His Kingdom to destroy the works of darkness in the world. When you yield yourself to Jesus, you allow God's Goodness to work in your life and in your relationships. Darkness does not want sinful people to be treated with God's Love and Goodness. And people unaware of their orphaned heart will easily fall into the path of the tree of the knowledge of good and evil. You will not be deceived by humanism when you seek God and are with Him daily. When you are close to His heart, you will know His ways. Submit yourself to Jesus. Surrender your heart and mind to Jesus. This is a challenge, but it is manageable because He is with you, and He helps you. You know that He will work with you to complete your transformation. The only thing you can do is focus on Him and let Him do His work.

When you are close to His heart, you will know His ways.

The reason you can do good is because the Goodness of God is in you. There is a process to move from humanistic goodness to heavenly Goodness. There are three essential works needed to make your spirit healthy as symbolized by the same process done in your physical body: detoxification, nourishing cells, and strengthening immunity. Spiritual detoxification comes by lie-busting, healing, and deliverance. Spiritual nourishment comes by regular communion with God. Spiritual immunity comes through the knowledge of God. All start and are empowered by the Goodness of God.

Yes, you will learn how God's Goodness works to detox, nourish, and immunize the spirit so that your spirit can be one with His Spirit. And as you go through your days' activities, He is with you, keeping watch over you. He will continue to teach you throughout the day as you stay focused on Him. Remember, pray in the Spirit all the time.

Yes, you will overcome evil with God through the Tree of Life and not through the humanism of the tree of the knowledge of good and evil. Surrender yourself to Jesus by focusing on Him. Fix your eyes on Him. Don't analyze your emotions and your thoughts. Don't focus on your emotions. Don't focus on people's sin. Don't focus on their mess. He is the God of order, and He does not accept disorder either.

You will always do the right thing at the right time when you walk closely with God. He wants you to succeed. He never wants you to fail in anything. That is His Goodness. By walking in His Goodness, you will have the same attitude toward others as He does because of His character in you.

Rest in God's Love and focus on Jesus. You are easy to work with when you trust in God and open yourself up to Him. Of course, there is some resistance in the flesh, but you can persevere through when your heart and mind are determined to follow Him. Your wickedness has to yield to His Goodness.

CHAPTER 6

YOU ARE CALLED TO CONQUER THE WORLD WITH GOD'S GOODNESS

Philippians 2:15 – so that you will prove yourselves to be blameless and innocent, children of God above reproach in the midst of a crooked and perverse generation, among whom you appear as lights in the world,

ONLY THE GOODNESS OF GOD can conquer the world. Man's goodness gives the devil the legal right to afflict man. It has never been God's intention to allow man's goodness to glorify Him. It cannot and never will. That is why Jesus told the rich young man, "Why do you call Me good?" The rich man was thinking of the humanistic goodness in Jesus, but He did not have it at all. As Jesus only said what He heard from the Father and did what He saw the Father did, then there was no way His good deeds came from humanism. Jesus did not operate out of His flesh, in His own will, and out of worldly wisdom. He totally submitted Himself to His Father's Spirit. His Goodness

It has never been God's intention to allow man's goodness to glorify Him.

came from His Spirit and not from His Soul, speaking in human terms.

In fact, He was complete with no separation between His Spirit and Soul. But for man, since they are not whole, there is a separation between their spirit and soul, and Jesus' statement revealed that goodness out of man's soul is dead because it is from the tree of the knowledge of good and evil. The goodness in your spirit that is one with and submissive to His Holy Spirit is the Father's Goodness. Therefore, in order to live out the Goodness of God, you need to pray incessantly in the Spirit and open yourself more to your connection with Him, giving Him more control in your life.

There is no deception in God's Goodness, and there is nothing that can counterfeit the Goodness of God.

In your past, you might have been hostile, critical, and unapproachable, but the Goodness of God covers all while working to remove all of them from you. The Goodness of God will show on your face, in your body, in your behavior, be revealed in your thinking, and shown in your feelings. The Goodness of God is everywhere, in every aspect of your life, relationships, activities, communities, careers, and ministries, because the Goodness of God presides over your relationship with Him. You will minister to people the way that Jesus did. You will no longer be influenced by earthly, natural, and demonic "goodness" and evil. The Goodness of God is your Sovereign Counselor that will assure you in His Truth. There is no deception in God's Goodness, and there is nothing that can counterfeit the Goodness of God. The Goodness of God will surely bring people to His Truth and His salvation. Any kind of goodness that entices you away from God is definitely not the Goodness of God. The Goodness of God is the Tree of Life. Any other kind of goodness that does not bring people to God comes from the tree of the knowledge of good and evil. That kind of goodness will lead to death with all the religions that it produces.

There is no relative Goodness of God. The Goodness of God is absolute. Either you have the Goodness of God, or you don't. Either you minister the Goodness of God, or you don't. Either you operate out of the Goodness of God, or you don't. You glorify God by the Goodness of God. You should never think of glorifying God by your humanistic goodness. This is the truth that will protect you from falling into the trap of pride. Anything from you, regardless of how "good" it is, does not glorify God, but serves to glorify you, and thus traps you in the abomination of pride.

The way to protect yourself from falling into the trap of self-righteousness is to focus on God. The way to protect you from falling into the influence of the world is to focus on the Goodness of God. You know God's good intention for you. You know His good heart for you. You know His good gift for you. You trust His good timing for you. You are refined to pure gold, a perfect diamond, and brilliant light because you choose to focus on Him, on the Goodness of God. You are protected from the roaring lions because you focus on the Goodness of God.

The Goodness of God does not cost you anything. Instead, the Goodness of God gives you everything. The Goodness of God assures you with His abundant Life. When you focus on the Goodness of God, you will surely experience abundant Life. When you are filled with the Goodness of God, you will not be afraid to do good to people. No one, no situation can intimidate you from living out the Goodness of God. There is power in the Goodness of God. There is victory in the Goodness of God. No king, no dictator, nor criminal can stand against the Goodness of God. No persecution, trauma, ritual, or abuse can stand against the Goodness of God. They will all crumble under the authority and power of the Goodness of God. No wickedness can stand before the Goodness of God. The Goodness of God is your promised land. Will you take such blessings? You should! You possess your promised land as a conqueror and not as a defender. The defender is prone to depend on the mercy of circumstances and people, but the conqueror takes control of situations and stands against all humanism.

God is pleased when you are bold to enlarge your vision beyond yourself. Yes, He will bless you with His Goodness. You will reveal and teach the Goodness of God to the world. God has prepared you for your destiny. You are not small. You are not powerless. You are not limited. You are not poor. Your Father in Heaven is rich. He is infinite. He is extravagant. He wants to bless you unconditionally like a father does.

You need to keep in mind, though, that however exceptional you are, if you move out of God's boundaries, you will forfeit God's Goodness. But if you stay in Him, you will be exceptional! God will not let you down. He will keep you successful because you trust in Him, knowing your own weaknesses and shortcomings. Your failure is not God's failure. But God's success will be your success. It is important to exalt the Goodness of God rather than focusing on the wickedness of the world. The one who wins your heart and controls your mind will be the one that takes over your life and determines its course. Will your life reveal the Goodness of God, or will it surrender to the wickedness of the world? God wants the first option for you, and when you faithfully choose to lose your life to gain His Life, you will fulfill your calling and destiny. It is God's Grace that gives you the desire to be transformed into the image of Jesus, but those who are locked up in the prison of humanism can't even comprehend this desire. When they focus on the insurmountable objections and look at the limitations of humanism, they only see impossibility and defeat.

Your failure is not God's failure. But God's success will be your success.

You are no longer the gate of hell, but you are now the Gate of Heaven, releasing His Kingdom culture of Goodness and Grace. You are not your own or of the devil, but you are God's. Yes, the devil knew your destiny, even before you were ever aware of it, and had tried hard to steal you from God and block you from your destiny. But he is losing you now. He is a loser. Keep him a loser.

You can have a successful, mature life when the Goodness of God reigns in you. Indeed, you will not be influenced or manipulated by the wickedness in the world. Judge all situations as a way of testing and revealing the measure of the Goodness of God in you.

You are to manifest God's glory to His Church and to the world. He will bless you with His wisdom, the ability to understand His wisdom, and give you the power to execute His wisdom in faith and with authority so that you can subdue the world with His wisdom. His Goodness is your Leading Wisdom, your Sure Companion, and your Secure Protection.

CHAPTER 7

YOU ARE CALLED TO MAKE GOD FAMOUS

Matthew 5:13-16 – [13] *"You are the salt of the earth; but if the salt has become tasteless, how can it be made salty again? It is no longer good for anything, except to be thrown out and trampled underfoot by people.* [14] *You are the light of the world. A city set on a hill cannot be hidden;* [15] *nor do people light a lamp and put it under a basket, but on the lampstand, and it gives light to all who are in the house.* [16] *Your light must shine before people in such a way that they may see your good works, and glorify your Father who is in heaven.*

YOU SHINE YOUR BEST LIGHT by displaying God's Goodness, which means God gets all the glory, not you. If your good works trap people in your praise, it means that your light does not come from His Light, but from your humanism. You can do good works out of your humanism, but they do not glorify God. That is how you identify and guard yourself from humanism, which is the same as "orphanism." You are God's and He is yours, there should be no separation between God and every aspect of your life. People must see that you are one with Him. That is how you shine your light, which is nothing less than God's

Light in you. This knowledge leads you away from pride into appreciation and praise of the Good God in you.

The main characteristic of God that distinguishes Him from the world and the devil is His Goodness. No one on earth can manifest His Goodness unless he or she is in a relationship with the Father. The Goodness of God is the perfect and definite indicator of a life with a true relationship with God. A genuine relationship with God will manifest His Goodness to the world. The purpose of every person is to manifest the Goodness of God. The Goodness of God is the source of Life, the river of Life, and it establishes the Kingdom of God on earth.

God's Goodness does not have evil thoughts against anybody. When you realize that you are more powerful and have authority in any situation, you will have no fear of people. Indeed, you are not afraid of their wickedness because God's Goodness overpowers you. When you stand in the position of the Giver of Goodness instead of the receiver of man's wickedness, you are no longer a victim... you are more than a conqueror. You will also release God's Goodness into any situation and into people's lives to drive out the darkness of wickedness in them. No one can stand rejecting God's Goodness. No one can stand denying His Glory. That is the power of God's Goodness.

No one can stand rejecting God's Goodness. No one can stand denying His Glory.

When you hate people for their wickedness, it reveals your fear of their power to hurt you, and this fear empowers the wicked to inflict pain upon you. Fear, hatred, and resentment empowers the wicked to be more wicked to hurt you. God's Goodness is your protection!

Your desire for God's Goodness is actually His desire to protect you and enable you to stand with the authority of a winner over—and not the victim under—man's wickedness. God's Goodness does not require you to suffer in order to wake up man's conscience. That is humanism's way. God's Goodness alone can do the work, to strike the light of conscience into their darkness. God's Goodness is much like the purity of a child without their vulnerability. Instead, God's Goodness empowers you to be a conqueror.

This is done for God's glory, but also to give you credibility. Your transformation is your testimony. Words are not enough; people have to see, and no lie can stand against your testimony.

God's Goodness empowers you to be a conqueror.

This is a long journey, but you are getting there with God. Know that all the accusations and shame you have endured are not in vain because nothing is wasted with God. You are precious to God, and He cherishes and values everything pertaining to you and your life.

Goodness means to love and to care for the welfare of others. God's Goodness always has good intentions toward people. You know God through His Goodness. How do people know you? Through your wisdom? Through your selfishness? Through your self-righteous arrogance and jealousy? Through your success? Through your failure? Through your devotion to God? Or through His Presence within you as they see God's Goodness in you? How do people know you is the question you need to consider!

You want people to know you through God's Goodness presiding and prevailing in you. What is hindering this? Likely, the problem is traces of humanism in you. That is why God keeps you mindful of it. He wants you to work on identifying it and removing it from you. Humanism is your enemy. Even though you may have been led and walking with His Spirit, God still wants you to be more aware of His presence and counsel in your life. Everything has been orchestrated so that you can have His full heaven supporting you in your journey of transformation. In essence, it is a journey of transforming your human choice to God's divine election. This is not easy work for you, but nothing is impossible with God. Remember, you do not fight the battle yourself. Instead, submit yourself to God and the battle is His. God is here with you, and God is here for you.

You are above this worldly nature. Look up to God and nothing in this world can affect you or influence you. Your mind is more important than your flesh. Keep your mind focused above this world where all their works will be destroyed by fire, but you won't.

The Goodness of God does not compromise with the flesh. The Goodness of God will consume the flesh until it is not seen any more. Stay above the flesh. You have God's full support, and He is with you. Nothing can destroy a mind focusing on God and a heart intimate with Him. Then the Goodness of God just flows spontaneously to you and through you to the world around you so that they would know that God is good.

> *Nothing can destroy a mind focusing on God, and a heart intimate with Him.*

You are called to make God famous. Will you take this challenge? Will you accept the call?

CHAPTER 8

GOD'S GOODNESS IN THE PRACTICAL LIFE

JUST AS YOU had been living with your enemies, which are anger, hatred, bitterness, unforgiveness, manipulation, and witchcraft, you will focus on switching your mind toward God's Love, God's Grace, God's Life, and God's Light. Receive His Love daily, every moment of your life. Live in His Love, eat with His Love, sleep with His Love, work with His Love, walk with His Love, drive with His Love, communicate with His Love, talk to people with His Love, read with His Love, type with His Love, study with His Love, and even take a shower with His Love. Saturate yourself with God's Love. Secure yourself with God's Love. God's Love is hovering over dark places in you, and you just have to direct your mind to Genesis 1:2-3, where He is speaking Light to your darkness, and then the darkness will be gone.

There is no reason why it is impossible for you to experience the Goodness of God through faith and in His faith in His Word. The Holy Spirit is living in you, and from your innermost being flow rivers of living water, and the water brings Life wherever it goes and to whatever it touches (Ezekiel 47:9). It gives Life to your mortal body by the power of resurrection (Romans 8:11). Just be patient.

God is resetting your DNA to join His nine strands of Justice, Judgment and Holiness of the Father, the Way, the Truth and the Life of the Son, Righteousness, Joy, and Peace of the Holy Spirit. God is all in with you because you are one with Him. You are nourished and you will live in love, joy, peace, patience, goodness, kindness, faithfulness, gentleness, and self-control (Galatians 5:22-23). That is how you become the ambassador of the Kingdom of God, the representative of His Goodness. He is in you, and His fruit is already in you. You already have love, joy, peace, patience, goodness, kindness, faithfulness, gentleness and self-control in you. All you have to do is to choose God.

Pray before you respond. Realize Who you will stand for. Be settled with Who you are standing with. The world is plunging deeper into wickedness, and you know very well that you cannot do anything to change it by yourself. The world is in desperate need of God's Goodness and Grace, and He needs people like you to save the world out of the darkness of wickedness into His Light of Goodness. Yes, unrighteousness is always wrong and unacceptable, but you cannot fight evil with your own unrighteousness. You destroy unrighteousness with God's Goodness and Grace.

Just as the sun rises and sets regardless of your mood, so is God's Love and His faithfulness to you. God's plan and calling for your life has not changed for a split second. He is with you on your transformational journey. He knows your struggles, and He knows your sincere heart toward His Goodness and Grace.

Yes, it is not easy to be the representative of God's Goodness in this wicked world; but even so, we need more representatives so that His salvation can reach this world. God knows your weaknesses, but He chooses you. Do your weaknesses decide His calling for you? No! So many people out there need God through you. Self-righteousness is your enemy. Humanism is your enemy. Fear of man is your enemy. Don't fall into their condemnation. Abide in His Word and rest in His Goodness and Grace. God's strategy for you is simple: Be still and know that He is God, wait for His peace and wisdom, and respond with His Goodness and Grace.

Your attitude toward others while asking for their compliance to your demand needs to be flavored with God's Goodness and Grace. You need God's peace and His wisdom so that you will not react wrongly to the wicked or to your enemy, the accuser. Instead, be still and know that He is GOD and respond with His Goodness and Grace.

Say to God, "I choose to BE STILL AND KNOW THAT YOU ARE GOD!" And then RESPOND WITH YOUR GOODNESS AND GRACE!"

Be mindful to breathe His name, YHVH, daily for your protection and transformation. God is with you all the time, and you need to be aware of that so that you can be strengthened with the knowledge of His Goodness in you and be empowered to face wickedness with His Goodness. Remember, you are not fighting against flesh and blood, but against spiritual wickedness.

> Ephesians 6:12 – *For our struggle is not against flesh and blood, but against the rulers, against the powers, against the world forces of this darkness, against the spiritual forces of wickedness in the heavenly places.*

Don't stop the Breath of Life coming from His Goodness.

When you breathe God's name, you realize His presence with you, and the devil sees that realization in you and he dares not challenge you. It is not God's presence that wins the fight because He is with you all the time, but it is your knowledge of His presence that defeats evil schemes against you.

1 John 5:4 – *For whoever has been born of God overcomes the world; and this is the victory that has overcome the world: our faith.*

Faith comes by the knowledge of God.

Your promised land is God's Goodness. God's Goodness is your promised land. Anyone who wants to enter his or her promised land has to conquer his or her Jericho first. Jericho represented the first tithe of the first ten cities conquered by the people of Israel. Yes, it will be the most difficult one to conquer and many have retreated because of its fortified, thick walls. It is the same idea as overcoming mammon to pay tithes. But if you cannot pay tithes, you can't go into your promised land. The tithe belongs to God, and He doesn't share it with you. Giving the tithe shows your absolute trust and obedience. It testifies that the victory is not by your might nor your power but by His Spirit. Humanism cannot win over mammon. Humanism cannot win over poverty. The tithe is not your enemy. Poverty is your enemy. The tithe does not condemn you, but poverty is proof of condemnation in your life.

There is only Goodness in God, and therefore there is only Goodness in you as you abide in Him, and He is in you. Breathe His Life to leave no room for death. Nourish your body by reminding yourself that the rivers of living water are flowing in you. Don't lose heart in your imagination. Your mind plays a major role in connecting you to the Kingdom of God. You come to God through your mind, and you know Him through your heart.

You come to God through your mind, and you know Him through your heart.

To ensure that your heart is filled with the Goodness of God, keep your mind on Him. There is no one good in heaven and earth except God, your Father in heaven. Your mind has been jumping everywhere but now it should rest on Him. Diligently focusing on God is how you can enter His Sabbath where you can rest from your own works. By diligently focusing on God, you will let His works flow through you naturally and all you do is what you see Him doing. By diligently focusing on God, you will let His words flow through you naturally and you just say what you hear Him saying. Then all you say and do will reflect His righteousness and holiness. Such righteousness is because you operate by His Kingdom culture and principles, and such holiness is because you come directly to Him, from Him and for Him only.

CHAPTER 9

THE CALL FOR THE CHURCH

THERE SHOULD NOT BE ANY doubt in us about God's Love for us when we dedicate ourselves to Him. He has chosen us to manifest His Goodness to the world through His Church. As the world plunges deeper into wickedness, the world desperately needs God's Goodness revealed through His Church.

How can the Church rise up and shine the glory of God? By the Goodness of God. The Goodness of God enables the Church to experience His Goodness and then manifest His Goodness to the world—all according to the structure, the strategy and the function of His Goodness.

We want to completely destroy darkness, deception, desperation, destruction, devaluation, and defamation. There should be no injustice and unrighteousness in our presence when we walk in God's presence. Demons must drop to their knees, darkness must flee, humanism must recede at our presence because we carry God's Goodness. No lie or deception can stand in the presence of God's Goodness. Instead, in the presence of God's Goodness, the enemies drop their swords, fall on the floor, and proclaim that Jesus Christ is Lord.

That is what the Church should be taught and should know. The Church is called to dominate the world with God's Goodness. That is her calling; that is her destiny.

There is no way the Church could win the world with humanism. Humanism is the pride of humanity, and therefore it makes them fall. Pride is anything that blocks people from being dependent on God. Pride makes people independent from God, and therefore it is an abomination to Him. Pride should have no place in His Church. Pride is the enemy of His Church. Humanism is the opponent of His Kingdom. We will not represent God's Kingdom with pride in us. Watch diligently against pride. Pride does not build; it destroys. Pride is the enemy against the advancement of the Kingdom.

There is nothing impossible with God. Do we think of ourselves as being the means we implement His calling for us? Or will He manifest Himself through us to minister to the world? Yes, He has chosen us to establish His Church of Goodness, saturated with His Goodness, empowered with His Goodness, and identified with His Goodness.

Let us be clear. This world is indeed filled with wickedness, and anti-Christ attitudes are prevailing in every organization, even in our churches. God does not deny the reality in which we live, but He has laid out His plan to build up His Church of Goodness upon it. How does His Church shine His glorious Light as the world becomes darker and darker? By pitting His Goodness against their wickedness. As we continue to focus on God so that His Goodness prevails in us over our flesh and over our humanistic ways of dealing with adverse situations, we can establish His Church of Goodness according to Isaiah 60:1-2.

Isaiah 60:1-2 – *¹ Arise, shine; for your light has come,*
And the glory of the LORD has risen upon you.
² For behold, darkness will cover the earth
And deep darkness the peoples;
But the LORD will rise upon you
And His glory will appear upon you.

Can the Church shine her light without the glory of God? No way. What is the glory of God other than His Goodness?

Exodus 33:18-19 – *¹⁸ Then Moses said, "I pray You, show me Your glory!" ¹⁹And He said, "I Myself will make all My goodness pass before you, and will proclaim the name of the LORD before you; and I will be gracious to whom I will be gracious, and will show compassion on whom I will show compassion."*

His Goodness is, indeed, His shalom. The simple definition of God's shalom is God's Goodness. His Goodness is an all-inclusive package. The world is covered by the dark cloud of wickedness, and people are hungry for God's Goodness. He uses us to establish His Church of Goodness on the foundation of this revelation that we receive. Remember, it is His project to use us for His glory and His salvation to the world. We need to focus on the Lord. We keep focusing on Him so that He can work out His plan through us.

Yes, it is very important to teach and to preach on this essential and crucial topic as the world continues to plunge into the trap of wickedness. People are drawn to evil in this world. The more their mind focuses on the evil in this world, the more they allow evil to develop and propagate throughout the world, even in God's Church. While the world endeavors to infiltrate the education system with corruption, "dragonism," and humanism, God's people have made His Goodness an irrelevant subject or a minor topic in this era of human history. Even though they try to focus on His Goodness, reality keeps them switching constantly to evil, and they fall into the trap of switching His Goodness into humanistic goodness.

This especially happens under extreme persecution that draws people's attention to their situations and their effort to trust God. There are scores of heroic stories of their hard-tried faith, of their severe suffering, of their steadfast perseverance, of their good deeds, of their generosity, of their agape love for their enemy, and of their willful forgiveness, but sometimes, it got to the point where it overshadowed the Goodness of God. There are countless heroic stories of Christian endurance under the enemy's cruelty and victim to their barbaric acts—but how much credit was given to what God did on their behalf?

Through extreme persecution, the devil has managed to trap people's mind in the tree of the knowledge of good and evil to focus their thoughts on their humanistic power and endurance more than testifying God's Goodness and His power to protect and strengthen and support and rescue them. When humanism is exalted, consciously or unconsciously, knowingly or unknowingly, it legalizes and worsens the evil persecution against God's people.

It is time for the Church to know the difference between the goodness of man (which is humanism) and the Goodness of God. While the goodness of man provokes even more evil, the Goodness of God snuffs it out instantly and completely. The presence of God's Goodness means the absence of the world's wickedness, just like where there is Light, there is no darkness.

The presence of God's Goodness means the absence of the world's wickedness, just like where there is Light, there is no darkness.

The Church shines by manifesting the Goodness of God to the dark world of wickedness. It is not about miracles and signs and wonders, which are obvious outcome of the Goodness of God. Our focus is on the Goodness of God, which cannot be used as deception to the world. God's people have to know the Goodness of God. They have to understand and experience the Goodness of God in their own lives. All the manifestations of the Kingdom of God have to be addressed to as the Goodness of God.

God wants to purify His Church from all the doctrines and philosophies of humanism, starting with people like us. People under tremendous persecution are trapped, focusing on the cruelty of the enemy and on His visitation to help them endure extreme trauma. Some are deceived in exalting self-righteousness, which gives the devil the legal right to attack them even more through his agents. All humanistic praise legalizes the devil's attack, opening doors for the roaring lion to devour them. When we consciously or unconsciously exalt self-righteousness, we are walking out of God's safe covering. The Lord is with us all the time to remind us and draw us back, because He knows our hearts. Wholeness is when our hearts and minds are one with Him. Wholeness cannot be achieved outside of

God. God gathers, but the enemy scatters. God brings unity, but the devil causes division.

God gathers, but the enemy scatters.

The Goodness of God brings unity to the Church. Preaching about unity, the benefit of unity, man's attitude and response to the Word do not bring unity to the Church. We need to preach and teach the Goodness of God.

The Goodness of God will expand on earth through the Church who provides anointed teachings of the Goodness of God. We don't have time to waste for anything else but to learn to walk with God and to know His Goodness.

Yes, there is so much waste…waste of time, waste of money, waste of resources, waste of people, and waste of energy to fight against the works of darkness instead of using energy to build up, to construct, and to edify. God's people are busy fighting against the wickedness of the world, but His Church does not have the essential that the world needs. We fight defensively instead of offensively because we don't focus on the Goodness of God, which is the only antidote to the wickedness of the world. There are so few teachings and preaching on the Goodness of God because God's people don't know the Goodness of God. They know the goodness of man, and so they fight based on the premise of the goodness of man. It is time for revolution in the Church to teach on the Goodness of God: what, why, how, and when.

We have to start the trend. We have to learn how to walk with God. Don't be distracted with other knowledge about how to minister to people. We are chosen to live out God in this world, to minister out of His flow. This is crucial and vital for all the Church's ministries. We must expose humanism and protect God's people from humanism. It is not easy to be free from humanism, but nothing is impossible with God. We need to learn to walk with God and live out Him so that we can totally defeat humanism in us.

God calls us to teach God's Goodness. As wickedness expands in the world today, nothing else is more important than teaching His Goodness to the Church. It is not about preaching to God's people that we must be good to the enemy. It is not about preaching to the congregation how to love the sinners while standing firm on the righteousness of God. It is about equipping the Church with the knowledge of God's Goodness, training her working out God's Goodness, and empowering her to walk by the Goodness of God to conquer the world.

As wickedness expands in the world today, there is nothing else more important than teaching God's Goodness to the Church.

When the Church does not exalt the Goodness of God, she will fall into the trap of wickedness that brings fear and resentment, which fertilizes and expands darkness even more. It is time to exalt the Goodness of God. It is time that God's people understand the Goodness of God, know the Goodness of God, and live out the Goodness of God.

God's Goodness is the ultimate goal for His Church. God's Goodness is her ultimate achievement and ultimate glory. The world is plunging deeper and deeper into darkness, meaning that it is becoming more and more wicked. God is going to flood the world with His Goodness through His Church to destroy them all.

How can we start this change? Make a serious survey of the status of the Church in relation to God and to the world. Is she glorious with the Goodness of God that the world runs to her to enrich her or is she shaking under the pressure of the good and evil of humanism that the world uses to corrupt her?

Consider the Word in Revelations 3:18:

> **Revelation 3:18** – *I advise you to buy from Me gold refined by fire so that you may become rich, and white garments so that you may clothe yourself, and the shame of your nakedness will not be revealed; and eye salve to apply to your eyes so that you may see.*

We have been taught and preached to a lot about a lukewarm Church. But what does a lukewarm Church really look like? Can we define a lukewarm Church? Surely a lukewarm Church does not glorify God and she is so unpleasant to His taste that He just wants to spit her out (Revelation 3:16). Why? Because she is carrying the distasteful goodness of man! She does not know the tasty Goodness of God, and she does not operate in the Goodness of God. It is time the Church recognizes that she is short of the Goodness of God. It is time that the Church recognizes that she is short of God's glory. It is time that the Church recognizes that she is poor, naked, and blind. It is time that the Church reaches out to God's mercy through His rod and His staff.

Revelation 3:19 – *'Those whom I love, I rebuke and discipline; therefore be zealous and repent.*

One of God's love languages is that, for those He loves, He rebukes and disciplines. He counsels us to buy from Him gold refined in His fire of purification so that we can become rich in His holiness. We should buy white clothes so that His righteousness can cover us from our shameful humanistic nakedness. And we need the salve of wisdom to put on our eyes so we can see the hope of glory, the glorious inheritance, and His unmatchable power to win the world through us.

Then and only then, to the world, the Church will shine God's glory, be the lighthouse guiding people out of darkness, and be honored by the world.

CHAPTER 10

GOD'S GOODNESS IN THE REALITY OF YOUR LIFE

GOD IS THE SOURCE OF LIFE, of Light, and of all the Goodness in the whole universe. In His Goodness, He has created you beautiful, bountiful, and powerful in His image because you are from His essence. He created you to dominate the world with His Goodness. You can run away from His Goodness, but you cannot stay away from His Goodness because you came from His Goodness.

The devil has managed to deceive mankind away from God, but he cannot deceive mankind from the awareness of Him. Regardless of how much darkness he has covered the world with, he can never block mankind from seeing His Light. He can never cover His Light; darkness can never defeat Light.

Through you the world will get to know His Goodness, experience His Goodness, and enjoy His Goodness.

In the Goodness of God, He has created you to be a treasure to His creation. You are His gift to mankind. Through you the world will get to know His Goodness, experience His Goodness, and enjoy His Goodness. His

Goodness is the Light to the world. People are walking in the darkness of wickedness. There is no goodness on earth that can overcome such darkness—except the Goodness of God from His Kingdom.

God is everything good from His Kingdom. God is good in creating you; God is good in redeeming you; God is good in restoring you; God is good in blessing you; God is good in equipping you and empowering you to succeed in everything you get involved in this world. God is good in protecting you and providing you to live on earth with the luxury and the majesty and the security of His Kingdom.

God is everything, every way to you, meaning that you lack nothing from Him at anytime and anywhere. That is Who He Is to you, and He will anchor this Kingdom stronghold in you so that all deceptive worldly strongholds in your life will shatter.

God loves to teach you, to coach you in life, and to bless your generational lines. God's Goodness is for you and your descendants. God loves to see you walk in His Goodness, righteousness, and justice so that you may enjoy Life and be a Life-giver to the world. God loves to see beauty. God loves to see prosperity. God loves to see you in freedom to live in His shalom. God loves peace, prosperity, and perfection in His Goodness. Life is flowing to you without hindrance or hiccup. You are free to receive the flow of His Life, and you are free to surf through this world with ease, skill, and victory. That is beautiful. That is how God's people must experience and live.

The work of Christ is powerful in every way to restore and reconcile everything to Him. Set your mind on the Spirit so that you can know Life, Peace, and nothing less than His Goodness that He wants for you. He wants to fill you with His Goodness. He wants you to fulfill your destiny with the fullness of His Goodness. His Goodness is your goal of living.

You are great because of God's Goodness in you. You cannot be anything less than who you are because of where you came from. You came from God's Goodness, from His greatness, and from His grandeur. It is by God's Goodness that you conquer the world and subdue the world to His will and His Kingdom's culture. God's Kingdom comes to earth through His Goodness in His people. Nothing less than God's Goodness will work.

Beloved children of God, God calls you to conquer in His rest because of His Goodness. You are not to fight in the chaos of humanism. Man's goodness forces you to fight against evil. But God's Goodness empowers you to conquer the world. The goodness of man fights heartily against wickedness, but the Goodness of God defeats it with matchless power.

Beloved children of God, you don't need the whole world to agree with you, but you surely need His approval of your every move. He has shown you how, so fix your eyes on Jesus, set your mind on the Holy Spirit, rest

> *The goodness of man fights heartily against wickedness, but the Goodness of God defeats it with matchless power.*

your heart on Papa's Love, Goodness, and Mercy, and fill your mouth with praise and thanksgiving to Him! By His Grace, ask Him to fill your mouth with such a good word of edification that, in due time, you may give grace to the hearers (Ephesians 4:29).

Be prepared for the outpouring of God's Goodness upon your life. He wants you to be His delegate of Life-giving to the world. It does not matter how much the devil hates you and has tried to stop you, you will overcome him and his schemes by God's Goodness. The devil has deceptively blurred your vision with your shortcomings, your ignorance, your mistakes, your weaknesses, your sins, your trespasses, your iniquities, and your family failures to block you from God's Goodness. But when you recognize his tactics and determine to focus on God, you open yourself to His Kingdom, and nothing can stop God's Goodness flowing into you, empowering you to conquer the world and fulfill your destiny as the representative of His Goodness.

God's Goodness should be the theme of your life and the foundation of your ministry.

God's Goodness should be the theme of your life and the foundation of your ministry. Your ministry should focus on the Goodness of God so that you may impact people with the Goodness of God. People will experience and manifest the Goodness of God. Evangelism focuses on showing God's Goodness and testifying His Goodness already operating in people's lives. Before you can show God's Goodness, you have to experience God's Goodness through detoxification, nourishment, and powerful immunity. Detoxification removes darkness from you. Nourishment enables you to know the Kingdom culture. Powerful immunity protects you from humanism.

You are covered in the Goodness of God. You are safe in the Goodness of God. When you are saturated with the Goodness of God, there is no wickedness inside or outside that can influence you. Your mind is the first gate to the Goodness of God—the open door for the Goodness of God. When you choose to focus on the Goodness of God, you welcome the Goodness of God into you and allow it to take control of your life.

Of course, you have been living with a carnal mentality that makes you prone toward humanism and the path of the tree of the knowledge of good and evil. But God is with you to help you overcome this stronghold of humanism. Yes, He purifies and restores your will to enable you to trust in the power of the Goodness of God and to do His will. It is not easy. That is why you need God. That is why He is here for you. If you could do it yourself, then that is the work of humanism. No work of humanism can help you overcome humanism which is the path toward death. The more you focus on God, the more you are prone to the path of Life and the steadier you walk in the Goodness of God. The Goodness of God is not your goodness, and therefore you don't naturally live it out. For now, you may naturally live out the goodness of the tree of the knowledge of good and evil, but that is your temporary desert experience until you move to your promised land, which is the Goodness of God.

In this world, you are nowhere among the elites, the good, the generous, or the philanthropes. You have no name in this world. Nobody knows you. You have nothing to bring you up there. But you have God. You have the whole Kingdom of God to back you up. You belong to God. You have no glory of the world, and that is a great thing. Your life has to depend on God totally so that you can shine

His Light to the world. The light of the world is darkness. But God's Light is the true Light, and there is no darkness in His Light (1 John 1:5). There is no darkness in the Goodness of God. You fight against all the wickedness of humanism in you by focusing on the Light, the Goodness of God, and trust its power to overcome wickedness. God's people fail because they focus on the wickedness of the world. They meditate on it, rehearse it, and exalt it. But for you, every adversary that comes against you is to train your will to focus on God and the Goodness of God. That's your weapon and your protection.

> *There is no darkness in the Goodness of God.*

The task is simple: focus, focus, and focus on God in all situations, regardless of how you feel. That is why it is so important to pray constantly in your spirit with the Spirit. It is vital to fix your eyes, not on what is seen, but on what is unseen (2 Corinthians 4:18) for the Goodness of God to live in you and through you.

When God's Goodness wins you, then you can win the world with the Goodness of God.